Acclaim

MW01074234

MAMA SAPPHO

ESCUCHE LA PALABRA... LIBRETE ESA!!!
Second poema and this is what is screaming silently in my head!

Joanna Galindo, Favorite Prima

Teresa Osa Hidalgo de la Riva's much awaited and timely poetry collection, *Mama Sappho*, provides ample evidence of the importance of critical witnessing for grasping the complexities of urban landscapes filled with racial violence, alienation, poverty, incarceration, social and academic dysfunction. Her poems outline the necessary elements of personal and collective survival and attest to an ever present ancestral homelands that forge a path toward a different kind of future filled with love, healing, and story.

In this collection poetry has an important role to play in this social transformation: it enables people to see through barracades, to generate inward impressions that cleanse and "show the world how to love again," "build and work in truth," and remember that a contract with unity is essential for any movement forward.

Angie Chabram, co-editor of
Speaking from the Body: Latinas on Health and Culture

This collection of poems, originally composed over 30 years ago, harken back to another era of sapphic love and chicana memory. Wrapped in cornhusks and smelling of califas central, these poetic morsels leave billowy trails of ritual smoke that follow the reader off the page. Read them and allow yourself to be carried over the mountains into the healing embrace of this curandera poet.

Juana María Rodríguez, author of
Sexual Futures, Queer Gestures and Other Latina Longings

In these early moving poems from the seventies, in which her "story was just taking shape," Osa reveals she has always been a powerful force, always demonstrating the strength of women. Or as she puts it, "a dark amazon barely unmasked" whose "warm shell has become molten." She also had a strong yearning for community, which was aroused by a "sweet bitter taste of home" and "strong pangs of homesickness for a destination yet unknown."

Marsha Kinder, Professor and Director
Labyrinth Project, School of Cinematic Arts
University of Southern California

"I never met her./ I always knew her." Osa Hidalgo de la Riva's writings represent the poetic journalism of 'back in the day.' Her words hold that "sweet bitter taste of home" we (queer and of color) recognize in our own hungry mouths. Do not forget this work. Do not forget the lives that made your lives livable.

Cherríe Moraga, author of
*A Xicana Codex of Changing Consciousness –
Writings 2000-2010*

Enigmatic and intimate poems. Deceptively understated and as fresh as when they were first published.

Lata Mani, Feminist Cultural Critic and Filmmaker

Her poetry isn't much, it's just everything.

Liz Hidalgo de la Riva, author of
Primitive and Proud, and *Phoenix*

MAMA SAPPHO

MAMA SAPPHO

Poems con Sabor a Caló

Dr. T. Osa Hidalgo de la Riva

Foreword by Angela Y. Davis

Kórima Press

Cover Art Title: "CENTRO de ARTE LOGO: Familia Mandala"
Artist: Dr. T. Osa Hidalgo de la Riva
Medium: Linoleum Block Print
Year: 1974

Author photograph: Dr. Bear's Selfie,
                   Austin, TX, Valentine's Day 2018

Book Design: Lorenzo Herrera y Lozano

Published by Kórima Press
San Francisco, CA
www.korimapress.com

ISBN: 978-1-945521-04-1

in dedication to the spirits of
my ancestors, y a mi familia
mestiza.

i pray only to share my work
mixed with undefinable love
inherited, with the many youth
i pass.

CONTENTS

III. LA FARSA

IV. HERESY

FOREWORD

It has been said that the creative genius involves the ability to lift one's private experiences to a level of universal truth through the particular art form one chooses as a mode of expression.

This collection of poems by Teresa "Osa" Hidalgo-de la Riva, is so enormously exciting because she invites us to enter her own inner world and simultaneously compels us to acknowledge our deep emotional solidarity with her feelings. A committed young poet, Osa Hidalgo-de la Riva knows how to articulate her subjective experiences in ways that urge us to explore new dimensions of our own lives. Should we not all want to "travel to a river we used to know"?

As a woman of color, Ms. Hidalgo-de la Riva refuses to believe that racism and sexism are eternal and unchangeable flaws of human history. Without resorting to superfluous rhetoric her poetry persuades us that social oppression can be constantly questioned and vigorously challenged, "...let us worry about children that grow old before their time, of young people dying and of old folks experiencing a rebirth from a bottle." Her love for women is expressed with such disarming tenderness that normal hardened prejudices against homosexuality swiftly dissolve.

Osa Hidalgo-de la Riva's poetry is permeated with a profound vision of hope—for finally indeed we will all "travel to that river we used to know."

Angela Yvonne Davis
Oakland, 1979

ACKNOWLEDGMENTS

On International Women's Day, 2018

this is the most difficult of tasks. it should be no wonder that this comes last, but not least. there is literally not enough room to acknowledge the beautiful familia, friends, teachers, people who have brought me to this point; who have lit the fires under my bear butt, in my eagle heart, and in my horse spirit that got me galloping and prancing all the same. i'd like to simply say, you should know who you are...blood familia and extended familia who took me by the hand with patience (most often), and love (siempre)...

mama lola angela, first and foremost. papa-san 'uncle lu' resting in power. my scorpion sister liz and brother louis. the virgo twins tim and laura. all of the beautiful next generation: trent marley cuauhtemoc, mia angela isabel, liliana maya, erin jaclyn mahina. dear tías celia y lucy, chepa y chole y chita. tíos gabe and kiki. grandma angie and grandpa frank. grandma manuela...

life cuzins: augie-san, gina y cathy, sergio, moraga y celia, marías (chávez, cortinas, cora), adriana y maritza y erendina, susy, marcia y cindy y wanda, lillian (castillo-speed, hellman), merle, lucha, nellie, mitsuye, chela, pat z, maylei y leis, eileen, chau y marcus, roban y estela, viva y sandra, chili d, carlita, lucrecia, loras, jp, juana maría, rosalee, chicana cris, emma, pedro dp, nancy, moctezuma, lenore, jeff, pam, rudy, jesús, nane y jenny, suzanna (sánchez, sampson), vane y danny, jenovah y rosa, rosamaría, rita y amina, orisha, jamila, ekua y rhee, beth, yreina, linda, anna, jasmine, laura (perez, guiterrez), madonna, ramona, georgina, mercedes, beva, kathryn y tracey y alma, silvia, auro-san y sandra, roya, crystos, lorna dee, harryette, bell, alma, patricia y rosanna, lupe y lorena, valentine y bill, luz y catriona, luis, jessie, orlando, patti and james sr, randy, raúl, blackberri, bionco y rey, nusrat, pratibha, lata, deena, isabel, yvette, tomás, roberto, adan, lito, paco, leo, nelson, dalida, nivea, josie, migdalia, mary lou, carla, lakota, odilia, dorinda, maya, pablo (álvarez, lynch), sally, wendy, victor (bautista, yañez), yolanda (lópez, noriega), rio, sarah, rené, malaquias, roz, krystal y kelly, lorenzo...

real cuzins: joanna, sarah, roberto sr "god's favorite vato," alicia "lil' mac," roberto jr, gabriela y maría, joaquin, lucio, frankie, tony, angie, karmen, liliana, yano, chente, derek, kevin, zachary, jennifer y j's, thaddeus, reggie...

life teachers: angela, jj, marsha, minh-ha, michael, sylvia, lourdes, todd, tara, doe, dolores, norma a, norma c, angie c, adaljiza, betita, chon, rosa-linda, fredric, ms hawkins, mr ulm, mr lee, ms chan, ms reese...

several-k students who cared and taught me también...

real inspiring orgs: centro de arte, gala, mujerio, curas, maldef, naccs, malcs, qcc-sf, dolores huerta foundation, barrios unidos sc, charlotte maxwell clinic, osher clinic, my womencare homies, the outsider fest crew, kórima press, gms, royal eagle bear productions c/s

rest in power: sister monica louise, tía lupe, tío amador, pat (gonzález, parker), june, audre, gloria, marsha, mauricio, john, chente, rodrigo, margarita, xavier, horacio, chata, virginia, debra, josé (muñoz, montoya), denise, bill, kathleen, carol lee...

and to all my loving relations and ancestors...

my most sincere gratitude and love.

INTRODUCTION: *CAN I RE-POSE*

Sunday, septiembre 24, 2017

Up on the third floor of el centro, downtown Santa Cruz, Califas, Aztlán, a lot has changed since the gathering of poems *con sabor a caló* of this *Mama Sappho* collection. Not sure if it is or has been a long time in coming, or even if it is early to the scene. That's something to think about, but I'll add that to the list of things to do for a later date. I'll recycle my lil' sister Laura's phrase, 'it is what it is.' And relax in the belief that these sentiments, memories and metaphors will reach hopefully welcoming hands and hearts when the time is ripe.

I am now the ripe young age of 63 minus a few days at the commencement of this Introduction. I was so much older then as the song goes–I was mainly in my twenties when my master's degree committee signed off. 26 to be exact. Some could say still wet behind the ears, or maybe ahead of my years with wildness. That's how this woman bear was be-ing as my other sister Liz calls it. The times were so different then. I had completed an activist artista high school life.

Coming out in southside Stocktone, while mama Lola was raising the baby twins born in 1970. We all eventually made our way to the urban roar of eastside Longo, where the Centro de Arte was to be community home of so many, many up and coming, down and going, brown and growing, multi cultural and sewing the fruits of so much creative labors of love. That was the commencement of a decade that tasted of, as they documented, affirmation and resistance all the same.

In 1970, I had my first bout with malignant cancer, and lived to tell about it.

Sunday, October 1, 2017
7am

The homeless woman on the street below awakens me, sonámbula. She hollers a stream of semi unconsciousness louder than her male counterparts. With good reason. The reason being that she uses her voice to defend herself from the preying dangers that lurk at every corner and penetrate her existence for decades or even millennium. She has more to wail about. Across the ages they will call her La Llorona, have you heard. If not, trust me that her memory echo these city streets reaching rooftops and the hearts of existing gods high up in the skies. Her feet gravitate to the center of earth reminding us that we have such a long way to go to reach our collective humanity.

In this day and age, Olmeca space-time witness affluent governments intentionally stalling, painting canvasses of genocide to line the halls of decadent ancestry. Portraits of mexicano, puertoriqueños, boriquen, taíno, caribe, xicanx, africano, maori y más children, women, and the rest who are not resting these moments expiring collectively under a banner of genocide. Some things never change. This poet turned 63 yesterday with the privilege and growing beauty of familia and friends, living and past, and even future. For real. And we were "be-ing" just that. Celebrating in the vein of creative resistance. *Siempre* in dance, laughter, tears, pain, good food, and music—potpourri of generational recall, really. And as it was in the myriad of metaphor buried and burned in ceremony amongst the lines of *Mama Sappho*. It is up to you to find them, to do the work and read between the lines, and hopefully continue to build our new and progressive tomorrow, from the ashes of our ever erupting here and now. Word.

Wednesday, October 4, 2017

It is the full moon and all of us female de la Rivas are pretty exhausted on this one. We threw down at this past weekend's Libran celebration. Liliana and I blew out candles in front of familia and friends at our little private bday celebration. It was a wonderful day and I have been having a wonderful week.

So now the intro of *Mama Sappho* is coming into fruition. I can feel it is under my fingertips. now, I need to track the changes I have made to the manuscript and send her off to have a world of her own. I am ready. As I dance across this keyboard, I love writing, always have, and probably always will. I am glad to study in the presence of mi familia. We learn from each other and continue to share our vulnerabilities, and support our duties to each other and to ourselves. We continue to encourage our own individual forms of leadership and commitments to our communities. We show the world how to practice unconditional love. And many people follow in our rhythms.

And as a seven-year-old I wrote in my first child poem with young pencil by the glow of the hidden flashlight under covers, literally, after curfew, in southside Stocktone:

now the night has ended,
the bright yellow full moon is shining so bright down upon me
and she seems to say, good night, sleep tight.
the trees around are standing so tall
they seem to protect me, I feel safe
...good night, sleep tight.

Friday, noviembre 3, 2017
full moon tonite

In one way, I want this to be a letter for my tía Celia, a nearly ninety-year-young butch identified be-ing who loves me dearly. For our love will be eternal. A mom-dad of sorts who was pretty much always there for me.

Before I started school, she was doing teachers college at San Francisco State ("College," then). It was the fifties and she and her kind had to pass codes to enter privado spaces to dance, drink, be merry and gay. Her Hawai'ian friends treated me like a doll when she'd bring me from Stockton to the rainbowed city. They'd sing and play their ukuleles so beautifully. Made me want to play. She taught me to respect books to the degree that I had to wash my hands and clean my fingernails when I held them. I can understand that, and not.

It is time for you to get what you can from these early poems. Or maybe they are too late. They are up for interpretation. They are poems built on the foundations of infinite meanings of metaphor. They lead into the heart, mind and spirit of open awareness of whatever twenty-year-young dark-skinned lower incomed enriched cultural street experiences can hold. She-holds. Heresy. Season songs of dark women. Califas amazons feeding bears and wielding shields of gold. Stringing orgasms and singing the lore of sapphos born of ancient Africa, Americas, and Asian persuasions. You can find these journeys between the lines of this collection, but then again, you may not find her.

5th de noviembre del 2017

Living on Capp and 24th en la Mission in the 70s—when my mission was to record the events, scents, colores, dolores of the day—was simply hyper sensational, to say the least. As a young, vibrant, dark-skinned chicana, xicanx-indígena dancing the streets of this hot flaming rainbowed San Panchita city was a pretty amazing scenario, literally and metaphorically.

The 70s were the years I met the likes and powers and beauty of many world womyn changers, shakers, and doers. More than all the above, it was a pre-SIDA/AIDS tiempo. Movements and rhythms were not only in the vein of resistance, they also shared the flavors of renaissance. Unless you've been there and done that—at this point under the madness of 45 – who's NOT my president—it's hard to explain. I can barely bearly take these vital moments of survival to reminisce and scribble a few pages or words working to form an INTRO to this collection, which originally began *WITH POEMS AS GUNS*, and morphed into *Mama Sappho*, poems con sabor a caló. Somehow, they have found their way into your hands.

A final message that Libran Ntozake Shange scripted in her revolutionary 70s choreopoem clearly, "for colored girls...let her be borne and handled gently."

> Can I re-pose this directive in such trying times,
> so many decades later?

I was a poet first, that was my first language.

MAMA SAPPHO

I. LA MUJER

IN FORMATION

soft bird humming bothers my ears. deliver me from evil.
type machine at onset of india dream. poetry of fury to
support thesis to support advancement of study. to what
degree is this necessary. she already told us why that
caged bird sings.

the world spins by in mayan breaking time. mother forgive
us. high strung instrument varnished beyond investable
honor. where are you identical twin. take me to the river
and pray for us.

to write is to right but to touch is a different story.
glory is buried in the tremble of professors fingering my
bookshelves. they call to deconfirm my emotionless state
flooded by some one word message.

weary from rapid rounds sung in unfamiliar tunes, my soul
stands in formation. high aim to justice fired last month's
meat i cannot eat.

mujer,

i have always questioned Giant Note Collectors, and
even more, Giant Note Senders. it has always been funny
watching what different ages do with time. we are definitely
silly animals.

have you been okay lately? part of my need to
communicate with you comes from some internal warnings of
your health; physical, emotional, mental, spiritual. i
hope you are still standing sure in your moves and your moves
being a safe speed and that speed giving you support needed.
i hope my worrying has been unnecessary.

i have a strong itch to move again. school is
everything i expected. it is wasteful, arrogant... a part
of my craving is being met -- being avoided. if this note
seems vague, it may be so. this time -- filled with papers,
assignments, lectures and poems -- seems to be as obscure. my
flying has taken a shift in elevation.

this note can easily become a book, pero, i struggle to
tell you the 'justs.' i miss talking to you, sometimes. i
miss seeing you, sometimes. i miss laughing and working
with you, sometimes. i miss the me around you, sometimes.
it is almost april and the showers have just begun.

HIDALGO DE LA RIVA

dear closet india,

i am making love to this morning bird that sings
outside my window cell of exile. my typewriter friend keeps
watch as we blast off to planets coming closer but not close
enough to meet. i am currently paying for formal training
in bypassing the emotions on the way to the theater.

my books are piling up un-red as I spend weak-day
afternoons attending old friends' funerals. evenings are
spent on intertribal lessons of feeling and form. my
mornings remain reserved for the bird.

TEQUILA RITUAL

I lit a candle
made an altar
prayed
put on my rings
took off my rings.
My fingers
each moment
nearly frozen.
Decided to give you peace.

I tried then.
I put on my mask,
took off my faith
went out on the city street
saw leaning gutters.

THOSE URUBAMBA DRUMS

Frightened by brick agency walls
Blond Winston 100 signs
Block my sun
Cover the only office window.

Urubamba drums beat louder.

For a moment
I thought I was watching
Some naked brown native child
Dancing.

Urubamba drums beat louder.

The native child ran out of my office
And climbed the nearest tree.
I took the next plane south.
I was told I went completely insane.

Urubamba drums beat louder.

I found along the way
A Terminal Island sister
A Wounded Knee mama
And my Bellevue queen.

NOTES TO MY ENEMY/LOVER

My world is distorted.

Everything is built on unevenness.
This decrepit mansion slowly tumbles.

You and I have always known what we could be,
Have always realized our limitations.

I should apologize for my rage
But my hands are still tied.

I am not articulate.

I can barely whisper the word 'love'
And pray that the wind may carry it your way.

HIDALGO DE LA RIVA

ZONE 4: A Prison Poem

Zone-4
Lunch time.
Send the patients down.
    Get your asses up
    Lazy bitches sleeping all day
    Put your make-up on
    Make your beds
    And hurry up!

Zone-4
No funds for the outing
Take them to Rap's Supermarket
Let them pick out a cheap Christmas tree.
    In line asses
    Let's all cross at once
    We'll take this tree
    These women are from the hospital
    Give it to them for free.

Zone-4
Visiting hour.
No passes for you or you.
    The ladies all get along here
    She is doing fine
    You have to be easier on her
    Virginia. give your family a kiss good-bye!

Zone-4
We know it is freezing back there
Our electrical system has gone hay-wire.
>God damn it,
>You'll just have to wait
>Until they fix it.
>Take that taped paper off those vents,
>Are you crazy!

Zone-4
The doctors are on their way
Patients in the TV room
For group therapy.
>All of you are to be in the room now!
>The doctors can't be waiting around for you
>And act right this time!

>>They took Pauline today
>>For the treatment.
>>Jean gets to go home tomorrow
>>But she really does not want to.
>>Dorothy is still crying.
>>Let's go switch beds again.
>>Stop making out with Maria.
>>Steal our charts so we can see them.
>>Meet you in the shower room.
>>The pricks won't give me any medication.
>>Try sneaking past the nurses' station.

What day is it anyway.
Write on the walls.
God damn, it's cold down here.

At night, I am scared to go to sleep.

SYBIL WAS A LIBRA

today i visited a poor woman. but then she might not have
been poor. others called her poor, in fact they called her
crazy too. now that i sit to think of it, she just might
have been you. before i sat down today i thought i knew what
i saw and now i do not.

before i awoke today i had terrible dreams. i had a
nightmare they told me. then i woke up. i saw my dreams.
maybe i never went to sleep. or maybe i have never been
awake. before i woke up i was sure i had a nightmare, and
now i am not sure.

before i started i thought i knew what i was doing, and now
i am not sure. but i do know that i will write to all my
friends.

HIDALGO DE LA RIVA

BETTY SCOTT

Betty Scott was a Black mother of four daughters. She was a
political activist who believed in intercommunalism, the
coming together of different peoples. She helped found and
was a teacher at the Inter-Communal Youth Institute in
central Long Beach. She was assassinated by the California
Highway Patrol.

I.

I am talking about two women.

The mama Betty
Was on her way to the City
The cops pulled her over
She reached for the registration
The cops blew her away
In her head, her strength.
She left four daughters,
The youngest nine months old
            One year ago.

            One night ago,
That baby daughter Naeema
Was carried away, stolen
In the parking lot of a supermarket
By two men. A man found
The almost two-year-old

Black mind and black body
Fifteen minutes later,
In a trash can, dead.

I am talking about two women.

II.

The news came after midnight.

Funeral arrangements must be made
Sixty dollars for county cremation and pickup
Petition for plain-clothed police escorts
For that baby breaking the front page
With familiar black blood ink,
For the baby behind juvenile bars.

III.

Can you hear her whispers?
        I never met her
        I always knew her
Can you hear her screams?
        I feel her soft breath in my ear
        I shall never walk the same.

II. BURIED WITHIN EACH FEMALE DEITY

SHE IS

we stay awake until the wee hours of the night because we
are free americanos. we can send women home. watch women
out our window of third story victorian existence. call
nineteen year old possibilities. drink tequila. dance.
sing. cry. make mistakes. grow. die.

la semana de la raza. we cruise the streets with the rest
of the cruising youth. she was not used to one night stands
even though we had already become a fourth or fifth. mamá y
la familia mestiza calls.

the moon has refused to become full. my dream content of a
play has moved away. las mujeres outside my window have
taken down their puerto rican blue curtains.

mi tía sleeps under a heat controlled casa. she knows she
has heard me if only for a second. la gente de la misión
know that they have heard me being serious. seen me being
for real. they know that they know that.

my mama needs a typewriter. she needs some income too. i
am on my way to the giant earthquake with my smith corona.
south where the land is quaking with my heart. why are
women so goddamned scared of women.

i have to fall asleep believing en la luna i slept under en
méxico. the one that promised protection. if i cannot
sleep, at least i will be able to understand.

i can fill up this whole white page because i write papers
now with ease. i stay up all night spending raza time
typing papers for white men until i get sick of all the
gringoness.

it is then that i desire to borrow the morning bird's wings
and follow the family of trees south. borrow somoza's gun
and turn it against him under este quinto sol. turn his
chest the color of the robin's.

SEASON SONGS OF DARK WOMEN

let me reach for this black book deep in the secret parts of
my room. love of putty that we wish to blend and form into
each other. let me indulge and give all. rise in flames
that i am unable to name.

we are shaped masochistic and carnivorous in this era. walk
masks and dance in frenzies. we have lost the beat of soft
barely rediscovered in momentary glances every other decade
we meet.

IN ACTUALITY

Not pessimistic -- reality.
Wind through the circles again
Recall a level higher up
Each memory more positive.
Not positivism -- reality.

One flies over the cuckoo's nest
By a shift in elevation.
No one understands my anxieties
Not even the producer.

I sleep in a room I offered to rearrange
By the light of an altar barely established
Next to a dark amazon barely unmasked.
I have been crying for two days.

Not masochistic -- reality.
Suffering the close of relationships south
The celebration of beginnings north,
Everything is relative -- everyone related.

We will meet again on some people's street
(I borrow lines more often now from previous poems)
And rap of perpetual rebirth through my tears.
Not masochistic -- reality.

Not sadistic -- reality.
I want to torture all
That caused confusion -- pain,
In the city of the fallen angels.

HIDALGO DE LA RIVA

dearest you,

my hope, i pray you are happy. see through every barricade
planted by the enemy lurking heavy on us, penetrating every
pore until we bleed, scream in rage, for silence and peace
created in each womb.

inward impressions will show the world how to love again,
build and work in truth. wash our faces. discard all
costumes. cleanse our systems and souls. pureness will be
fed by our songs and stories.

our contract is unity against that beast that devours our
children and sends women home bruised and marked with
blemishes of tattoos and degrees.

we will travel to a river we used to know.

MAMA SAPPHO

window of heaven
mounds of califas
scattered in a soft blue ocean
connected to that lavender horizon,
forest of baby clouds sleeping.

what brush painted these skies
composed this singing sea
what poem does the stillness carry?

MAMITA, WHAT ARE YOU COOKING?

Tree of life seasons
My emotions, the sea.
My blood sprays the sky crimson.

The gods of hell fire
Bake young canned heat.

Inkwells control rainclouds
Faults are placed to purify las montañas.

ALL READY

my new friend, my old lover, that we should be left to daily
routines of things *ms*pelled and memories of this parade we
march in.

girlie whoremonia you tell all, and i give all through
silent emotions. we release a pair of dice past scars of
loss. we are young they tell us over and over. forget
those bridges we set afire at the onset of yesterday's
nightfall.

brave enough to open chests buried during war. there are no
words left, only gold and rubies ready to be strung.

we believe in crafts and building. we believe in surviving
and crying hard when slaughter comes to collect. we paid
dues at birth. if only visions were seen in the four sacred
colors we share.

my weakness, my twin, that we should learn to know this. a
strength that men would build revolutions from. we cannot
turn back when forces call time during a time we wish to call
our own.

when pow wows and romance are in control we are foolish to
discuss januarys and semesters. the evening star smartly
took us by our venus hands.

HIDALGO DE LA RIVA

BURIED WITHIN EACH FEMALE DEITY

Imagine love, all these secret coded messages we cannot even
    decipher.

Let me come immeasurable times to you in poetry and whispers
    on haloed keys of
Onyx instruments in melodies never heard. we are as ancient
    as a rare
Vessel created and buried within each female deity. modeled
    to comfort
Even a patriarchal prisoner long forgotten and tortured.

Yesterday we rehearsed tunes without color and spice. now
    we try and tame
Our desires. improving as we see each day shed tears and
    shells of us.
Unfolding to each other and to the world.

TO YOUR GROWING COLLECTION

to the one that would take all these libraries,
i add one more song to your growing collection.

pride is a rusty word being oiled.
wells run dry

and there is no space or time allowed
to ask why we continue.

goodnight to things in all directions.

sleep well with my name as soft on that
beautiful mouth as on my newly discovered tongue.

if i could control these phrases
without your flesh each day

i would cap the flow and swim
in all that has escaped me already.

III: LA FARSA

LA FARSA

enter free people in the minds of kings and queens of the
streets. reyes y reinas de nuestro turf. civilizaciones de
niños llorando cuando los actos comienzan.

drafted audience community organizers take their scarred arms
and minds needled with bitter smack to exist behind a dormant
cell. back drop high on a city hill overlooking a curtain of
bars, supporting kleenex when plots are discovered.

housewives cast ballots. vote telenovelas en vez de
estaciones de documentales. volando escapando. ordenando
ropa sucia. back stage delicacies fermented saturate el
viejo con su salsa brava.

i question now if chains are made únicamente por el macho. i
watch man-made women offer children to intermissions.
prisoners control concession stands. todo el nonsense has
been collected and is feeding and growing.

y los gringos are left to build reviews. columns erected on
a synthetic syndicated foundation. instant reality cooked,
made ready to feed twenty mutant children at the battered
women's shelter in an alley adjacent to the theater.

evening contemporary world poets, sonámbulos, take their
third seats quietly to sleep in museums of decadent european
ancestry. relegated to wipe castles of sand blown glass
filled with urine specimens and materials from the waste
land.

SHOW TIME

ten minutes before show time. city terrace holds the key to
my cell. try and sell me more mocos y ascos and i will be
just that. i believe we can have the world on platters, gold
as popped corn, vibrator humms as ample as on and off switch
movement if we close our eyes and jump.

seven minutes before the curtain. i leap into your arms and
vast sea as i have too many times before. be strong. grow
and break a leg is the best advice i can give. it is hard to
be an indian these days.

look at all the cagada we revise five minutes before show
time. when our play has ended and that bright yellow full
moon that shone on my first poem offers us marriage will we
refuse her. will we choose cultural events over parties.
choose natural juice over booze. choose political parties
over each other. will we. can or should we.

young and foolish we stand in the dressing room and watch
mirrored play rehearsals. stars were we, is what we will say
when we age. tempt me to bind you in the women cords
inherited for umpteen years and carry you to freedom.
ironic. strange.

city terraced sunday stroll on hollywooded avenues. she is
all my fantasies and fears. see her into nirvana and
oblivion without any errors.

HIDALGO DE LA RIVA

STREAMS OF SEMI-CONSCIOUSNESS

the moon on my left ear is aching. dreams were left behind
on the secret ship to a dingy midwest prison. bound for
higher degrees of verse. i greet mistakes that validate a
cynical lookout point. too much emphasis is placed on each
word and phrase. no regrets nor excuses as juke box advances
the unfamiliar tunes. up dream in pan vision multi colored
talkies. i should not ask for any more when you call from
that mean city. mamie, long captured in jars of jelly and
butter and unable to throw arms up bandaged in splints.
pero mamie, where is there left to return to.

strong pangs of homesickness for a destination yet unknown.
i await your letters every so often. i pretend that i
receive them and respond sacredly as often as twice a week.
where would we be without senses. since mine are so
polluted i seek a location to trade them in. i will tell
our emotions as soon as one is discovered. somewhere at the
end of youth and the beginning of middle age i want to give
up. i heard if poets make it to forty they usually live
outstandingly long lives. forty seems so far away.

i am tired of streams of semi-consciousness. of ladies
sailing away with my heart. of giving, taking and lying to
be loved. can one really believe a poetry haven exists
in a state no one ever mentions. have they heard of califas
and east los en iowa? i am so afraid without due ammunition
that i may be captured. our armies have not formed tight
enough for my records to be watched by our guiding mothers.
unless i find her here within time.

always returning to the silly farces of life, death and all
that shit. have to be or nut books are ever incomplete.
sing a happy song the radio blares. i sit and stare at
rainbows purchased over the counter. they hold the mysteries
to that past sold in the shape and name of crystallized blue
persuasions. running to the bathroom for comfort, i realize
that i am sick.

DEEP SOUTHERN STYLE

ladies crying over dinners.
mamas dying giving birth.

how do you carry scars
planted at youth?

memories of ketchup smells,
odors of animals
run over.

deep southern style
de califas central.

sweet bitter taste
of home.

ABOUT THAT AGRI-BUSINESS

I saw pink devils
fertilize what they thought should grow.

The mass.

On Sunday the Mass was read in English only.

In Stockton, the version is modern,
K-mart style.

Traditionalists
tried only to sell
at fruit stands and corner markets.

THE STING

I.
She picks the dice with grace
With ease.
She shakes her fist too long.
She casts a spell
With a climax so familiar
To those who compete.
She rolls a perfect score.

II.
He was a 300 pound won ton soup eater.
Asian and short in stature
The man had soul.
He also knew how to roll.

III.
Both sat stunned
Not knowing who won
Or even why the game had begun.
They left the player's table
Satisfied yet frustrated
As player is taught to be.

MACHO

an ex-lover
defined this as
the phenomenon
of males

trying to imitate
the natural strengths

of the female role models
they see.

HIDALGO DE LA RIVA

FINALS

this journal is up. my notebook is complete.
this term is over. i am sick, rundown and tired.

i have let everything go. held only to silent ranks.
i want to lament a bright colored oval shape
contrast a huge blue sky.

can you help me find my way home?
long behind wooden desks
my legs and mind are too cramped for running.

caldo caliente became an entity of the past,
y amor a common verb.

i sought all semester a space to sleep,
an hour of undisturbed sacrificial study,
a pair of comfortable walking pants.

i enlisted in an army of color blind writers
amputated below the third eye.

i yelp after classes, till moons shut off. creative life
cannot water trees hardened with beaten bark. i learn not
to remember that i am on the road to las pirámides via oz.

MAC, BEYOND SOLEDAD

and how could forty thousand years sift through my hand like
grains of sand weighing less than an ounce. when they
disconnected our first conversation via bell, i muffled a
what the hell if we grow so old before our time. this is the
only evident crime.

how you came, reaping silver dagger, and tore into my
existence. caught me in a frenzy whirling cycles of
transcripts, papeles and records we share, matted in my hair
like a madwoman this generation has not yet felt. why do we
cry so far away from each other's grip. why can i feel you
looking over my shoulder.

every time i leave that tiny apple, cuidad de divino san
pancho, i stare hard. he, lit up like some lit up woman on
a street tempting me, teasing me to join. growing smaller at
each interval until he tries to crawl up my feet.

ah. then you call. long distance it will read on next
month' s bill. we stumble for words, when all the words come
forth like troops to follow mi corazón. they halt at the
tip of my tongue and then we are told it is time to go.

you, sweet primo, are worried about me. let me be worried
about you. or let us worry about children that grow old
before their time, of young people dying and of old folks
experiencing a rebirth from a bottle.

HIDALGO DE LA RIVA

IV: HERESY

THE BEAR WENT OVER THE MOUNTAIN

if anything, one giant cycle is near completion. language
and appearance change. at times i feel more like wilde's
fantasies, hellman's maids or billie's clowns -- to wake to
lines marking new ages, marriages and movement.

if anything, my typing is much better, my singing more
clear, my head more sure in accepting all my indecisiveness.
i can run away and laugh in my rawness, can give thanks for
all the strength. actually, feel pretty good about how
this hell will turn into love.

one more cycle shell battle star galactica may the force be
with ye and all that trivia. nonsense while the beat goes
on. time seems to be such that it is hard not to ask you
questions but to tell you that i have warmed and exercised
my fingers in finding so many answers.

new babes grow into old witches and old witches into
curanderas y curanderas solderas y solderas sing to you
each hour before the rise of the storm. it is better to
learn with openess. i am finding out all stories end in
glories or tears. years are just the stuffers, money the
tease, laws and rules and regs to keep the toes on the line.
being strapped to this wheelchair is not so hard to look up
often and madly laugh.

books, poetry and cancer grow to protect my cells of
loneliness. are there no nuke words to watch and guide when
everything is built on unevenness and shale. where in the
hale did my toys and drugs go. whoremonia bed comes to
taunt and tantalize.

a seventeen year old vata loca homegirl gay and shining
rests in nightmares in a psychiatric ward after having
attempted to take her life, they tell me. but they never tell
me where in the hell she was trying to take her life to.

all these years of institutions i have been forced to sit
hours listening to billie shake his spear telling the
assholes something they never listen to. pendejos refuse to
allow visiting passes for me to return home. our time will
come though when time will tell. ironies and dramas will be
nothing more than the variety of colors in a pansie.

HIDALGO DE LA RIVA

DE LA RIVA

my mother would sketch on bar napkins
my grandfather would carry tiny pencils
as he jotted poems from his twelfth story gutter.

my warm shell has become molten
with anxieties and frustrations,
tries to be the victor of my needs and desires.

i want not to write
in standard upper class
academic english.

i am in méxico doing laundry in a stream
with some women i cried with this morning.
i am waiting to die to be reborn again.

NOTAS

I.

tonight may have been the night that i silently begged
to my mind's own alleys, kicking empty bottles and cans.
read, don't buy.

some giant powers surround las pirámides.

who are the children
that grow old before their time.
¿sabes tú?

believe it or not, i am still capable of feeling.

take me de la mano a la mañana.
use the ink until it runs dry.
my poems have always been foreign to you.

HIDALGO DE LA RIVA

II.

contradictions in this jungle.

to curse a woman hanging above the altar in her room,
to throw the nearest stone and crack her off the wall.

the birds and trees are on our side,
the boys in the band and the girls in the glee club lost.

she-holds are far apart
she felt for boys
saw her hang up her shoes.

i am still young and defiant
i don't want to find someone else.

III.

my home of coffins,
victims of the night and deadened memories
take heed.

the baby in the next house keeps crying and crying.

we act like children running naked in the forest.
my story is just taking shape.

when there exists a disbanded matrix
the exterior falls apart.

the bodies burn.

HIDALGO DE LA RIVA

AFTERWORD

Dear Reader,

Well, I wanted to begin this discourse, this immediate task of writing an Afterword to *Mama Sappho*, in the form of a personal letter, because this level of writing is more primary, basic, informal and direct. For survival purposes, as a world traveler woman, I trust this type of **talk** or **discourse** most. On the other hand, in the world of academia and private patriarchal towers of highest education, I desire a hybrid mix of lingo, siempre.

For survival purposes, the level of the personal transforms within the geographic political historically specific **self**, into the un, **sub**, **meta** and **supra** modes of consciousness. This is why I find it necessary to speak in a more **common language** first. In respect to the immediate task I've chosen, I am also curious to develop a reasonably sustained creative thesis that would contribute in a progressive way to overall world thought and culture.

At the same time, I walk a tightrope balancing act to stay true to so many values, her-stories, and languages at war with what is compulsory world knowledge indoctrinated/permeated within U.S. public schools as what is supposedly true world democracy and history. So what about **OUR** story? Maya Angelou already told us **Why that Caged Bird Sings**. Yet, I know in my heart, and with my blood, that something is wrong with this picture.

Caló, **Ebonics** and other forms/modes of linguistic mutations, alternations and transformations are readily accepted in this treatise/poetry collection. The occasional use of ancient **flor y canto** will be encouraged as a coping strategy to deal with the harsh realities of living in occupied **Aztlán**, realities that are seldom forgotten within the discourse of this 1970s Master's Thesis from San Francisco State University–*Mama Sappho*.

WHAT'S at STAKE for ME?

In this mode of self-conscious experimentation with form and content in this project, I intend to remain playful with the seriousness of proper Queen's English. I reckon if necessary, I could argue further for this attempt to rupture and challenge limits and boundaries of academic discourse (university/universe/ universal knowledge) vernacular. As a teacher in numerous social institutions, I have discovered that the bridge between the highly literate and the growing epidemic of world illiteracy is one of the immediate crises for which higher academic elitism is directly responsible.

Nevertheless, for survival purposes I understand the importance at particular times to stay metaphorical, evasive, and subversive in language. Subcultural icons of meaning that need to stay free from the confines of too rigid rules and regs custom-made to protect, serve, and feed hegemonic world culture censors. Dick Hebdige offers a pointed explanation of how these subcultural meanings come about to subvert dominant paradigms – and simultaneously how global capitalism continues to rapidly subsume/consume any original attempts through the commodification of popular cultural symbols and fetishes.

Language is a most basic form of symbolic meaning and for relationships of how consciousness is represented in both thought and culture. For example, for some, Alice in Wonderland didn't stop burning her bra and punching her pillow. And for Others, **Alicia en Aztlán** couldn't find **"enuf"** to pay the bills, feed and clothe the kids.

Personally, what motivated me to accept this mission, this task, this gift of writing a creative thesis—and now to publish it four decades later—, is that I am very interested on both micro and macro levels in a **mujerista** aesthetics and activism. On the micro level, I am interested in how Chicana artistas have individually created and survived as women artists, and how these works have helped create audience/spectator positions that generate a diverse range of responses. At this level I take the liberty to interject my own experience as part of another generation of **xxxxicana** poet/film/video/media makers, whose works reveal an array of productive similarities and differences.

On the macro level, I wish to understand how Xicanx lesbiana artista/poet/film/video/media-makers function and survive as cultural producers in a particular moment in history—the contemporary realm. Of major interest is the dialectic of how their works have already influenced and can continue to influence the shaping of particular cultures and how those cultures have influenced and shaped these media-makers. On this level, current local/global, socio-economic, personal and political dimensions are collectively understood. For example, I am concerned with the question: "Is there a Chicana aesthetic?" And, more particular, "Is there a **mujerista** aesthetic?" If so, what is the difference between these two, that is, between Chicana and **mujerista** and their respective aesthetics?

The first time I heard and recall registering the concept **mujer** was in the late '60s and early '70s as I came into my own Chicana consciousness. As a child, my papi took us via long hot road trips from **south side Stocktone**, **Califas**, to his borderland hometown of **Del Rio, Tejas**. I heard from tíos and primos that **mujeres** were to stay at home in the kitchen, cleaning, cooking the next meals, doing laundry, and taking care of the smallest children. My dad, however, allowed his girls to go fishing with the men. Even the preparation for this outing was a big event: getting bait and tackle, picking up all the fisher-men and boys, throwing them in the back of the truck, getting ice, snacks, and finally, last but not least important, gassing up and getting enough cervezas. I soon realized that once the camp was set up and the fishing lines were cast, these men spent a good amount of time drinking the tons of beer they had brought. And regarding the role of women, after watching the men after their "hard" day to bring home the fresh fish, I learned of the different privileges traditionally allowed Mexican men but not women.

The border between gender roles didn't make that much difference at the time. I was so proud and thankful that my father didn't enforce the same rules for my little sister and me. He allowed us a choice between staying and working at home with the women, or joining in on these fishing excursions.

Once, I decided to stay with the **mujeres** because there was a cousin who was just too sweet to me. Still, the day was torture. To me, all the work the women did was by far more laborious than what their male counterparts were up to. Not only that, even though I had a language barrier, being that English was my first and only language at the time (and I was still having problems with that European language, probably still am in certain circles, let alone the romantic Spanish language), from what I could understand, the women basically preoccupied themselves with a different type of chat I wasn't too happy with. They talked about the men, the boys, the children, gossip about other women, children, and families–things that didn't seem too interesting to me.

Many, many years later, in **lesbiana** San Francisco I heard of and joined a group called **MUJERÍO**. For a while, one of my sisters and

HIDALGO DE LA RIVA

my mother were also members. I always wondered why a group of radical political Latina **lesbianas** would use the traditional Spanish masculine gender ending **MUJERÍO** for a group that consisted solely of females. I had heard that in proper patriarchal Spanish if there were a room of a thousand females and one single male, they would be described as **ellos** as opposed to the majority of **ellas**. Of course, that dynamic rule of grammar was not applied the opposite way. Basically, in Spanish language, males rule. I tried to change the name of the group for political reasons having to do with the sexism of the language, but the other women wouldn't have it. To keep peace within myself I tried to understand it in terms that we were all so strong, and in a traditional patriarchal mindset, our **lesbiana** dynamics were as powerful as "men." If not, then even moreso, when considered in relation to a synergetic whole. Nevertheless, I continued to call the group **MUJERÍA**. Many of the **mujeres** would laugh it off saying it was the creation/mutation of an English-only-speaking Chicana; I was once again only warping the Spanish language.

By applying this term **mujería** to mediamaking praxis, I demonstrate our investment in the ways in which philosophical beliefs and practical implementation by women and mothers of color have advanced the idea and struggle for a better tomorrow through the raising of our children. Within these specific works I attempt to decode, give the 411, size up, check out and rap about the daily findings of my surrounding world of the 1970s. By representing our-selves in arte, we can begin to heal the damage done through misrepresentation and under-representation. I wish to explore the ways self-representation in literature can lead to healing via community building and self-empowerment, and more specifically focus on the importance of X^xicanx^x poets as **mujerista mediamakers**.

CYBER CAFÉ COMMUNICATIONS
Morelia, Michoacán, México

I am interested to see how historical events have created circumstances whereby Chicana filmmakers can do their work. I am equally interested in the content and poetics of these women's productions as well as their contextual situations. At the same time, interest in these external films and videos are relevant to the films and videos I internally envision. In understanding my own desire to create, I realize my creations have been fed by a **familia's** legacy of **Chicana/o arte** productions and activism on my Mother's side of the family. Women in my family have **cuentos**, contemporary ethnographic **testimonios** of cannery workers and working in the fields. As an example, and for the sake of **testimonios**, my own mother as young Chicana **artista** in the San Joaquin Valley taught arte at several regional migrant camps with youth in the mid 60s.

In more recent her-story, during these past few decades various younger women are forgetting important cultural- political events that were "before their time." For example, my mother was involved in several cannery strikes in Stockton, California, which were not documented. White feminists such as Robin Morgan, in her classic **SISTERHOOD IS POWERFUL** anthology, addressed some of the socio-political organizing that was taking place with women during the late 1960s and early 1970s in the U.S., during the second wave of feminism (but not as many women of color were documented). I would like to briefly share the multiplicity of levels at work in understanding this evolution of a **familia de artistas**.

My grandfather, **abuelo** Gabriel Francisco and my grandmother Angela's brother, Domingo Rubio, helped form a Latino literary organization in the San Francisco Bay Area in the 1920s. My grandfather was a poet and it has been said that he wrote a wide range of verse, which unfortunately has mysteriously disappeared over time. **Abuela** Angela was said to have painted at some time in her life and taught painting on a small scale from home. Co-founder of the **UFW**, Dolores Huerta tells me a **cuento** that she and one of these grandparents' eldest daughters, **mi tía** Lucy, actually had a social club while in high school in **Stocktone, Califas**. For several dances, they had their young guy friends carry one of the only console radio/record players from my grandparents' home across the train tracks on foot to the party place. I found that story hilarious.

Youth will do nearly anything to party–across all times and places. At the writing of this, I am in **Morelia, Michoacán** where many of the Rubios have lived for many generations. Domingo Rubio II, Angela's brother was Presidente Municipal, mayor of this capital city in 1939 and was involved in many socio-political affairs. This side of the **familia** had many politicians, educators, and organizers. My father's side came to California as farmworkers from Texas. My dad, like many other Latinos in the U.S., served in the U.S. Armed Forces; he was as a sergeant in the Korean War. He retired as a postal worker receiving an honor for a perfect driving record for over forty years. He was interviewed and televised as one of Stocktone, Califas' first postmen to drive an electric mail truck.

In the 1970s **tía** Celia took a silk screening course from Malaquías Montoya. The content of the art piece is political and privileges the **UFW** struggle, icon, and colors. **Tía** Celia also self-published a book of "gay woman's prose and poetry." But it was mis abuelos' youngest daughter, my mother, Dolores Angela "Lola," who followed arte for a majority of her life.

It is from this **familial** legacy that I have desired to create in film/ video production, which, of course, is a combination of the creative writing spirit of **mi abuelo, mi tía Celia, mi abuela** y **mi mamá's** strength in various visual and literary mediums. All my siblings, both brothers and both sisters, are wonderful **artistas** in their own right. I have had the honor to incorporate their creations in our **mujerista movies**.

At a **lesbiana encuentro** I was invited to speak at in México City, I was asked whether I believed "**Aztlán**" was real or a myth. My response: Both. My experience living in East Los Angeles reaffirmed this thought time and time again. There are many others that feel the way I do. "Nation" and "home" are as vital to fight and die for, as it is to sense the illusion of such concepts in relation to a **universalist** perspective. The violence of patriarchal history perpetually reconfirms the idea that I am indeed invested in the notion of **Aztlán**, in the collective political unconscious of such brothers as Alurista's poetic ode regarding the Aztecs and their ancient homeland "to the North." Nevertheless, at the hand of our own **familias** we have been oppressed, in the same vein in turn to internalize our own multiple forms of oppressions.

As sisters Pat Parker and Audre Lorde endowed future generations with the power of feeding spirits nearly broken, we must continue to question our pains, while singing a song of unconditional love. "How do we break these chains laying strange?" chanted Parker.

In the early 70s, during the origins of the predominantly white women's studies department at California State University at "**Longo**," I organized a women's cultural week/nite with women musicians Margie Adams and Vickie Randle. I was honored as well that Pat Parker came to read poetry. On the evening Parker joined

HIDALGO DE LA RIVA

us, just before I brought her to campus, she told me to grab some of my poetry, which I had previously shared only with her, close friends, and **familia**. She said she wouldn't read publicly that evening unless I did also. It was only a few hours before the show was to begin! I was forced to perform my first public poetry reading, and realize today what a blessing her considerate action was. I am so thankful in one way or an-other, that Pat Parker "brought me out," in this creative public performance **nueva onda**.

In retrospect, I realize the importance of encouraging other sisters to share their artwork with others as well. Voices that seldom are heard and experiences that are rarely given space and time to be expressed is what most liberation movements dealt with during the advent of the Civil Rights Era. Today, victims are encouraged to speak out, to assist in the process of healing. In East Los Angeles, I had the privilege to encounter and encourage many young Chicana/ Latina sisters to find access to newer technologies, film, and video— to tell, to yell, to sing, to dance, to cry, to write their own stories—by any means necessary.

We must keep face and strength before all elements of oppression, and finally, we must learn through a humane and loving practice, how to transform our contemporary dis-eased socio-political and environmental reality into one of health. Paulo Freire's method to teach literacy was to use elements of the native common language and recognition of common sounds and words. To teach literacy leads to knowledge, self-determination, and empowerment. There are so many rhetorical questions to ask in relation to why it is that human beings have remain in states of war, headed via chaos into massive forms of destruction. May this current treatise join in solidarity with a long line of radical struggle.

WHY is this CREATIVE THESIS IMPORTANT to CULTURA NOW?

I heard a talk/discourse by rapper D when I visited Harvard University for a graduate student of color recruitment event. Introduced by Professor Cornel West, Chuck D spoke about the importance of "**HIJACKING THE MEDIA**." He explained that behind every corporation there are individuals. These lessons of not to give unnecessary power to entities that we know little of, are also taught in the 1939 film **THE WIZARD OF OZ**. That is, that many of the people in power positions, as we discover of the wizard in the plot of the journey to Oz, are merely human like us, and that it's really no big deal to negotiate at various levels. This fear is demystifying people of color's involvement in otherwise white male centered arenas.

As women of color, for example, living in America and dealing with Anglo/Eurocentricism and male dominated corporations, systems and other state apparatuses, we must understand the reason for **culture shock**. When two oppositional forms of consciousness interact, there is an array of possible outcomes. These dynamics may include appropriation, integration, hybridization as positive, negative, and at times, I believe, even neutral energy forces. These experiences happen at both micro and macro levels of human evolution and re-evolution. With respect to issues of living healthy and striving for global democracy, this project also includes a self-reflexive archaeology of my-self (mind, body, and creative spirit). I do this to keep aware of my own positioning as poet, filmmaker, video artist, educator, and cultural critic. I do this to evaluate simultaneously a her-story of our neo-tribe, re-inscribing ancient wisdom with the flow of a pen—or a cyberspace wave. This is a contemporary ethnographic deconstruction of a highly technological mutant virgin puta hybrid culture continually being

HIDALGO DE LA RIVA

reborn. In an age of a cosmic race, la **raza cósmica** reconstructs newer visions of utopia–in an otherwise dystopic late patriarchal postmodern pathological disorder. This is a simple and yet highly technological song written in freedom and bound to the rhythms of the rainbow.

Lastly, this creative thesis is a passage of change for a **xxxxicana**-identified woman learning to master the queen's language, and the king's logic. And as it was in the beginning and as it is at the end of this **Fifth Sun**, for example, experiencing what is healing for the U.S. **lesbiana de color**. This pedagogical journey also has both a micro and macro level: as a personal one that I am following and as the basis for an alternative curriculum for transformational transcultural awareness. It is in this interplay between these two levels, that I find the importance and potential healing power of **mujerista mediamaking**.

Almost any alter-Native attempts at positively progressive change are exciting in this day and age. In this space and time, I observe and feel as both ethnographic participant and observer in this study. A transcultural human cosmology remains in my political unconscious and as crystal clear as an ancient **lengua** nearly lost. In the magic of survival at hand, at the forefront of creativity, as important parts of a whole **Chicana/o**, **women's**, **lesbiana de color**, **Movimientos**, the beat goes on. It is in the rhythm of these drums that I continue to follow.

To end this document, my bear senses warn me that I am electronically connected–flying on a cyberspaced symphony of dancing keys. Unfolding the dramatic landscapes of the heart, molding into a story, simultaneous purposeful and aspiring towards a universal void and universal responsibility. From the depth of a multidimensional, multiethnic, multisexual, multigalactic, multimedia expression out come these pouring words to you. In the goal of an Afterword I am constantly evolving into the synthesis of this transcultural space-time, I cannot but help **rite** these words away, from the least, and from the most, at an honorable purpose towards progressive and maybe more often than not, radical experiential stance and sensibility. For these reasons of survival, I am granted the freedom of this **POETIC PULSE**–and for all this, and more, and forever in the tune of loving all my relations, **con safos, y qué.**

APPENDICES

PUBLICATION RIGHTS

I hereby reserve all rights of publication, including the
right to reproduce this thesis in any form, for a period of
three years from the date of submission.

Signed: _Ms. Teresa Ann "Osa" Hidalgo de la Riva_ Date: _May 9th, 1980_

APPENDIX I   65

MAMA SAPPHO: POEMS

Teresa Ann "Osa" Hidalgo
San Francisco State University
May 1980

A collection of poetry and prose poetry con sabor de
caló.

MAMA SAPPHO: POEMS

A creative work submitted to the faculty of
San Francisco State University
in partial fulfillment of the
requirements for the
degree

Master of Arts
in
English

by

TERESA ANN "OSA" HIDALGO

San Francisco, California

May 1980

CERTIFICATION OF APPROVAL

I certify that I have read MAMA SAPPHO: POEMS by Teresa
Ann "Osa" Hidalgo, and that in my opinion this work meets the
criteria for approving a creative work submitted in partial
fulfillment of requirements for the Master of Arts degree in
English at San Francisco State University.

William Dickey
William Dickey
Professor of Creative Writing

Kathleen Fraser
Kathleen Fraser
Associate Professor of Creative
Writing

Carol Lee Sanchez
Carol Lee Sanchez
Chair of American Indian
Studies

APPENDIX IV

TERESA de la RIVA and friends

BENEFITS

POEMS as GUNS

CALENDAR of POETRY and MUSIC

OCT. 26th
Saturday
9:00 p.m.
A LITTLE MORE
San Francisco
(Salsa night. With two Puertorriqueña poets)

NOV. 4th
Saturday
7:30 p.m.
RISING MOON - WOMEN'S CENTER
Santa Cruz
(With Naomi Quiñonez)

NOV. 9th
Thursday
8:00 p.m.
$2 donat.
LA PEÑA
Berkeley
(With Naomi Quiñonez, Lorna Dee Cervantes, Elizabeth de la Riva, Bernice Zamora, and música by Lucía Gallegos)

NOV. 11th
Saturday
7:30 p.m.
INTER-CONNECTIONS BOOKSTORE
Santa Cruz
(With Naomi Quiñonez)

DEC. 2nd
Saturday
8:00 p.m.
$2.50
THE GOOD FRUIT CO.
Santa Cruz
(With poets Lorna Dee Cervantes, Elizabeth de la Riva, Naomi Quiñonez, and música by Cacki Gates, Tish Sainz, Pat Smith and special guest Rita Lackey)

1977

CERTIFICADO NUMERO _____

LOS SUSCRITOS CERTIFICAMOS QUE EL SEÑOR

Manuel de los Reyes

QUE LEGALMENTE ADMITIDO COMO SOCIO ACTIVO DE LA

UNION OBRERA HISPANO AMERICANA

EL DIA 3 DE SEPTIEMBRE DE 1922.

P.M.I.

BERKELEY, CALIF, SEPTIEMBRE 3 DE 1922.

Pte.

Domingo Rubio

Sro.

Miguel H. Gama

APPENDIX IV

Celia de la Riva Rubio

Lágrimas y Cadenas

Chains and Tears

Poesía y Prosa Feminista y del Ambiente
Gay Feminist Prose and Poetry

Bilingüe, Español e Inglés
Bilingual, Spanish and English

Morelia, Mich., México, 1994

About Dr. Osa Hidalgo de la Riva

Dr. T. Osa Hidalgo de la Riva is an internationally renowned filmmaker, public scholar, and writer. Holding three master's degrees in Film Production, English & Creative Writing (both San Francisco State University), and History of Consciousness (University of California at Santa Cruz), she received her Ph.D. in Cinema and Media Studies from the University of Southern California's School of Cinematic Arts. As a post-doctoral fellow, Dr. Eagle Bear, as she is also known, taught *Erotic Women of Color: The Case of Hollywood* and *Sexuality, Gender and Media* in the University of Southern California's Critical Studies Division. From 2008 to 2013, she taught *Ethnicity and Race in Contemporary Film* at the University of California at Berkeley and in 2012 was the recipient of the Chancellor's Public Scholar Award from the University's Ethnic Studies Department.

Dr. Hidalgo de la Riva's films include *Mujería (part I): The Olmeca Rap*, *Mujería (part II): Primitive and Proud* (both formally distributed by Women Make Movies, New York), and, *Two Spirits: Native Lesbians and Gay Men* (Third World Newsreel, New York). The *Mujería* films debuted in San Francisco, CA, at the Kabuki Theater and Roxie Cinema, respectively, and attracted capacity audiences. "Las Olmecas," Dr. Hidalgo de la Riva's animation artwork, was selected to be part of the award-winning *500 years of Chicana Women's History/500 Años de la Mujer Chicana*, edited by Dr. Elizabeth "Betita" Martínez. Dr. Eagle Bear has lectured and spoken at numerous film festivals, seminars, community centers, and universities throughout California and nationally, as well as internationally in México, Canada, and Europe.

—La Osita
age 26

OTHER KÓRIMA PRESS TITLES

Amorcito Maricón
> by Lorenzo Herrera y Lozano

The Beast of Times
> by Adelina Anthony

Brazos, Carry Me
> by Pablo Miguel Martínez

Broken Mesas
> by Joseph Delgado

The Cha Cha Files: A Chapina Poética
> by Maya Chinchilla

Ditch Water: Poems
> by Joseph Delgado

Empanada: A Lesbiana Story en Probaditas
> by Anel I. Flores

Everybody's Bread
> by Claudia Rodriguez

Las Hociconas: Three Locas with Big Mouths and Even Bigger Brains
> by Adelina Anthony

I Love My Women, Sometimes They Love Me
> by Cathy Arellano

Jotos del Barrio
> by Jesús Alonzo

Lay Your Sleeping Head
> by Michael Nava

The Possibilities of Mud
> by Joe Jiménez

Salvation on Mission Street
> by Cathy Arellano

Split
> by Denise Benavides

Street People
> by Michael Nava

Tragic Bitches: An Experiment in Queer Xicana & Xicano Performance Poetry
> by Adelina Anthony, Dino Foxx, and Lorenzo Herrera y Lozano

When the Glitter Fades
> by Dino Foxx